dare to dream

dare to dream

thoughts to inspire success

edited by jo ryan

Published in the United States in 2007
by Tangent Publications
an imprint of
Axis Publishing Limited
8c Accommodation Road
London NW11 8ED
www.axispublishing.co.uk

Creative Director: Siân Keogh
Editorial Director: Anne Yelland
Designer: Simon de Lotz
Production Manager: Jo Ryan

ISBN 978-1-904707-57-8

9 8 7 6 5 4 3 2 1

Printed and bound in China

about this book

This beautiful little gift book is guaranteed to motivate anyone needing a lift in their personal or professional life. Its inspirational collection of thoughts, phrases, and mantras puts the value of trying as a means of success centerstage. Full of praise for those who try, keep trying, and do not give up, as well as those who work hard, and accept setbacks as opportunities, it will offer a quick pick-me-up and prove a handy reference for rainy-day moments. These words show that you should forget what's happened in the past, because the present and, more importantly, the future are bright and full of promise.

Complemented by a beautiful collection of amusing and cute animal photographs, these thoughts and sayings are guaranteed to hit a rich vein with people of all ages and from all walks of life.

about the author

Jo Ryan is an editor and author who has been involved in publishing books and magazines across a wide variety of subjects for many years. From the many hundreds of contributions that were sent to her from people from all walks of life and all ages, from around the world, she has compiled a collection to celebrate and foster success.

The hardest
victory is the one
over yourself.

Success and
rest don't sleep
together.

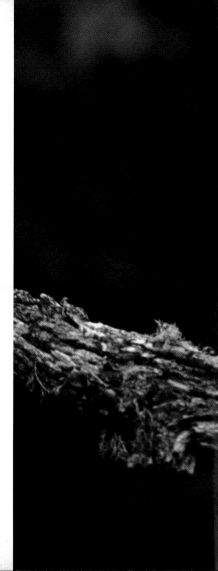

Look things in the
face and know them for
what they are.

Success depends
on effort.

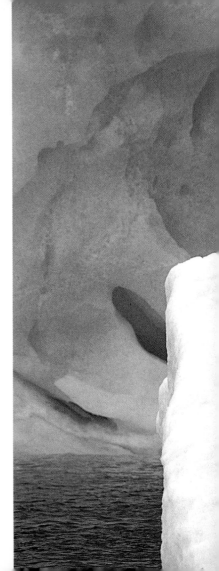

If things do not turn out
as you wish, wish for them
as they turn out.

Nothing is an
unmixed blessing.

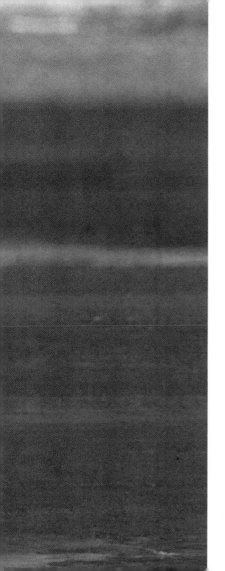

Footprints on
the sands of time
are not made by
sitting down.

In life the honors
and rewards go
to those who act.

Never let up.

Dare to be
remarkable.

Happiness is the meaning
and the purpose of life,
the whole aim and end
of existence.

On your journey to greatness, you must remain focused.

Nothing is certain
until you try.

Winners never quit and
quitters never win.

Success comes to those who are too busy to be looking for it.

You are born to succeed, not fail.

To win without risk is
to triumph without glory.

Your determination
to succeed is more
important than any
other one thing.

Blessed are the flexible, for they shall not be bent out of shape.

Never undervalue what you are.

The journey
is the reward.

It's a rough path to
the greatest heights.

Do what you
can with what
you have.

Hope is a
waking dream.

Tomorrow is often the busiest day of the week.

Don't look for success…

…it's so close you can reach out and touch it.

To laugh often and much is to have succeeded.

Dreams create
the future.

To accomplish
great things, we must
act, dream, plan, and
above all believe.

Vision
without action is
daydreaming.

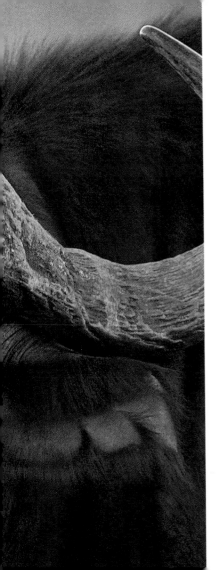

The dictionary
is the only place in
the world where
success comes
before work.

Sooner or later
the person who wins
is the person who
thinks he can.

Never be afraid to
go too far, for success
lies just beyond.

The only person who can cheat you out of success is you.

Happiness is the key to success.

Success is a
result, not a goal.

Great works are
performed by
perseverance.

Count your
age by friends
not by years.

You are here to
enrich the world.

To become a winner,
perform as though you
were already a winner.

Success comes in cans,
failure in can'ts.

You can't help
another without
helping yourself.

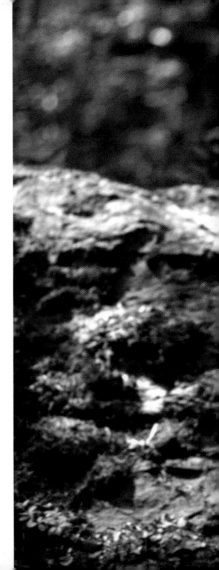

Don't think "problem,"
think "opportunity."

All men have
one goal: success
or happiness.

Good things come
to those who hustle
while they wait.

Imagination
rules the world.

If your children
look up to you, you've
made a success of
life's biggest job.

To be a winner,
all you have to give is
all you have.

Success is
nothing but luck.
Just ask any failure.

The ultimate
value of life depends on
awareness and the power
of contemplation.

Behave toward your friends
as you wish your friends to
behave toward you.

What lies in our power to do, lies in our power not to do.

You control
your own destiny.

The only limits
are those of vision.

Real knowledge is to know
the extent of one's ignorance.

Success will find
you if you give every
day 100 per cent.

Think like a man
of action, and act like
a man of thought.

We learn by doing.

If you don't know where you're sailing to, no wind is favorable.

Success is simple: do what's right.